NATURAL WORLD

POLAR BEAR

HABITATS • LIFE CYCLES • FOOD CHAINS • THREATS

Malcolm Penny

RSVP®
RAINTREE STECK-VAUGHN
P U B L I S H E R S
A Steck-Vaughn Company

Austin, Texas
www.steck-vaughn.com

NATURAL WORLD

Chimpanzee • Elephant • Giant Panda • Great White Shark
Killer Whale • Lion • Polar Bear • Tiger

Cover: Eye-to-eye with a polar bear
Title page: A bear peers out from woods in Cape Churchill, Canada.
Contents page: Stretching up to get a better view
Index page: A bear enjoys a playful roll in the snow.

Published by Raintree Steck-Vaughn Publishers, an imprint of Steck-Vaughn Company

Library of Congress Cataloging-in-Publication Data
Penny, Malcolm.
Polar Bear / Malcolm Penny.
    p.   cm.—(Natural world)
    Includes bibliographical references and index.
    Summary: Describes the habits and behavior of polar bears during the different stages of their lives, as well as threats they face and efforts to protect them.
    ISBN 0-7398-1060-X (hard)
    0-7398-1816-3 (soft)
    1.Polar bear—Juvenile literature.
    [1. Polar bear. 2. Bears.]
    I. Title. II. Series.
    QL737.C27P376 2000
    599.786—dc21   99-32666

Printed in Italy. Bound in the United States.
1 2 3 4 5 6 7 8 9 0 04 03 02 01 00

Picture acknowledgments
Bruce Coleman Collection 6–7 (Mr. Johnny Johnson), 7 (Joe McDonald), 14 (Mr. Johnny Johnson), 15 (Fred Bruemmer), 18 (Staffan Widstrand), 20 (Tom Schandy), 23 (Fred Bruemmer), 28 (Mr. Johnny Johnson), 29 (Staffan Widstrand), 31 (Mr. Johnny Johnson), 34 (Mr. Johnny Johnson), 35 (Staffan Widstrand), 36 (Fred Bruemmer), 39 (Staffan Widstrand), 41 (Fred Bruemmer), 44m (Mr. Johnny Johnson), 45t (Staffan Widstrand), 45m (Mr. Johnny Johnson), 45b (Staffan Widstrand), 48 (Fred Bruemmer); Bryan and Cherry Alexander 1, 3, 8, 12, 13, 16, 17, 21, 25, 26, 27, 30, 33t, 37, 38, 42, 43; Digital Vision 40; Oxford Scientific Films 9 (Norbert Rosing), 10 (Norbert Rosing), 11 (Norbert Rosing), 44t (Norbert Rosing); Still Pictures 22–23 (Philippe Henry), 24 (Klein/Hubert), 32–33 (Joel Bennett), 44b (Philippe Henry); Tony Stone Images *front cover*. Artwork by Michael Posen.

Contents

Meet the Polar Bear 4

A Polar Bear Is Born 8

Hunting for Food 18

Leaving Home 28

A Fully Grown Bear 34

Threats 40

Polar Bear Life Cycle 44

Glossary 46

Further Information 47

Index 48

Meet the Polar Bear

The polar bear is the largest carnivore living on land. It lives in the freezing cold climate of the Arctic, close to the sea or on the sea ice. Its thick, white coat acts as camouflage in the snow, as well as keeping it warm.

Coat
The fur looks white because it reflects light from the snow. The hairs are actually transparent and hollow. They are waterproof and trap air to keep the bear warm and dry.

An adult ▶
polar bear

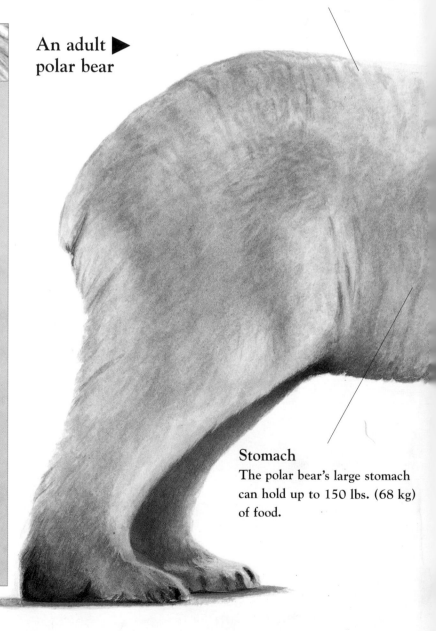

POLAR BEAR FACTS

The polar bear's Latin name, *Ursus maritimus*, means "sea bear."

•

A polar bear can run at 30 mph (50 km/h) on land or ice, but only for short distances.

•

The biggest polar bear ever recorded, in Alaska in 1960, measured 11.12 ft. (3.39 m) from nose to tail (the length of a small car) and weighed 2,209 lbs. (1,002 kg).

Stomach
The polar bear's large stomach can hold up to 150 lbs. (68 kg) of food.

The top of this map shows ▶
where polar bears live in the wild.
The red areas are land, and the
shaded areas show areas where the
sea freezes over to form ice.

Skin

The polar bear's skin is black. This helps keep
it warm because black absorbs more heat than
any other color. Under the skin is a thick layer
of fat, or blubber.

Ears

A polar bear's ears are small,
so that they lose less heat.

Eyes

A polar bear has no eye-
lashes (they would collect
ice), but it has a third
eyelid, called a nictitating
membrane, to protect its
eyes against bright light.

Nose

A polar bear has a very
good sense of smell. It
can smell a dead whale
from almost 20 mi.
(30 km) away.

Feet

The soles of a polar bear's feet are covered in fur,
so that it can move silently without slipping on the
ice. Its claws are very sharp, to grip its prey. The
bear's toes are partially webbed to help it swim.

The World of the Polar Bear

Polar bears live all around the Arctic, wherever there is ice on the sea. Although they spend most of their time on the ice, they are excellent swimmers. They can swim for many miles from one ice floe to the next. Their waterproof coats and thick layers of fat enable them to float easily. They can also dive underwater for as long as two minutes.

▼ Polar bears gather on a frozen lake in Manitoba, Canada.

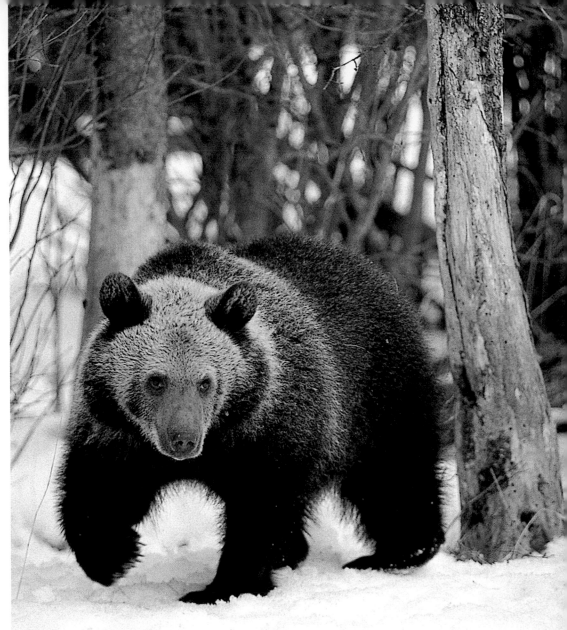

▶ A brown bear emerges from hibernation in northwest United States.

The polar bear's closest relatives are European brown bears, and American brown (or "grizzly") bears and black bears, both of which live in North America.

Its other relatives live in tropical forests. They are the Asian black bear, which lives from Iran to Japan, the sun bear of Southeast Asia, the spectacled bear from western South America, and the sloth bear, which lives in eastern India and Sri Lanka.

A Polar Bear Is Born

Polar bears mate in April or June, and the females are pregnant from six and a half to nine months. In November, a pregnant female polar bear digs a den, usually in a snowdrift. At the end of a passage 6 to 20 ft. (2 to 6 m) long, she makes a chamber where she will stay until spring comes. Some females use the same den year after year.

▼ A female polar bear roams the edge of the ice on the coast of Svalbard, Norway.

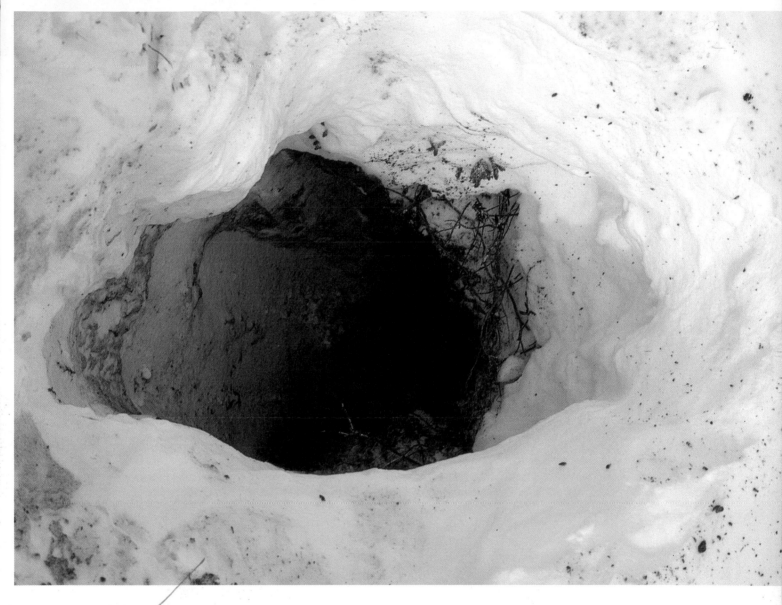

Although female polar bears stay in their dens for four or five months, they do not really hibernate. Their hearts slow from 70 to about 8 beats per minute, but their temperature and breathing stay near normal. Animals that hibernate can take several days to wake up, but a dozing polar bear can wake in an instant.

▲ The entrance to a female polar bear's breeding den. This is where she gives birth to her young and keeps them warm through the winter.

Birth

The cubs are born about six weeks after the female enters her den. There are usually two cubs. Sometimes there is only one, and very rarely three or even four. The newborn cubs are tiny—about the size of rats—and they weigh 20 to 25 oz. (600–700 g). They are blind, deaf, and completely helpless.

▲ These twin cubs are only about ten weeks old.

Although it is warmer in the den than outside, the temperature still falls below freezing. The mother keeps her cubs warm by cuddling them in her arms and by breathing on them. She feeds them with her milk, which is very high in fat. The mother does not feed at all. She lives off the fat she has stored in her body during the summer.

▼ Newborn cubs drink milk from their mother's four teats as often as they can.

POLAR BEAR CUBS

Polar bear cubs open their eyes when they are about thirty-three days old. They start to hear after twenty-six days.

●

The cubs stay in the den with their mother until March, when they weigh 18 to 26 lbs. (8 to 12 kg).

Into the White World

By March or early April, the cubs have grown to about the size of small dogs. The male cubs are already slightly larger than the females. The chamber at the end of the tunnel starts to get quite crowded. The cubs are quite happy where they are, feeding off their mother's milk. But their mother is beginning to feel hungry.

▼ A young cub plays with its mother, shortly after coming out of the den.

Finally, the mother breaks out of the den, pushing the snow away and poking her head into the air above. She must watch out for male bears, which might kill her cubs so that she would be ready to mate again. When the mother is sure that there is no danger, she climbs out onto the snow, and the cubs follow her.

When the cubs first see the huge, white world outside their den, they play and slide in the snow, rolling and tumbling with their mother. They will return to the den for a week or more to sleep, but now the open Arctic wilderness is their home.

▲ A polar bear family relaxes in the great white wilderness.

13

Walking to the Coast

The cubs are still feeding on their mother's milk, but her stores of fat are almost used up. She has gone five months without food, and she is thin and very hungry. If she does not feed soon she won't be able to produce enough milk for her cubs. She has to take them to the coast, where she knows she can find food.

▲ The cubs usually follow their mother in a line, but if the snow is very deep and soft, they run alongside her so as not to fall into her deep footprints.

The family might have to walk 12 mi. (20 km) to the hunting grounds. The mother bear could walk all the way in one journey, but her cubs are too small and weak to travel all day and all night. She stops every few hours to feed them and give them a chance to rest. All the time she watches out for male bears.

▼ While the young cubs sleep, their mother keeps watch.

Protecting the Young

Female polar bears take very good care of their cubs and defend them against any danger. They usually stay clear of adult male bears, but if one threatens her family, a mother can drive off a much larger male.

There are two reasons for this. The first is that she is very fierce when defending her cubs. The second reason is that a male dare not risk getting injured in a fight. If he cannot hunt, he will starve to death.

▼ This mother has driven off an attacking male, but her cub has been badly injured.

▲ An alert mother sniffs the breeze for the scent of danger. She always stays alert to protect her cubs.

If there is not much food available for a long time, hungry mother bears have been known to kill their cubs and eat them, in spite of their natural instincts to protect them. Young, inexperienced mothers sometimes do the same. The mother's instinct to survive is stronger than her instinct to protect.

MOTHER BEARS

Polar bear mothers have been known to rear up and leap at helicopters carrying research scientists, to defend their cubs from the noisy intruder.

●

If a mother polar bear loses her cubs, she will sometimes adopt others. One tagged female was found with a different set of cubs from those that were with her a few months previously.

17

Hunting for Food

Polar bears feed mainly on seals. Ringed seals are their favorite, followed by bearded seals. They also catch harp and hooded seals and sometimes scavenge on dead walruses and whales.

When she has cubs with her, a mother catches adult seals for herself, and young ones for her cubs. The cubs lie quietly on the ice while she hunts, waiting for her to bring their food. When they are older, they will follow her, gradually learning to find food for themselves.

▲ A cub waits patiently for food while its mother watches for a seal to come up for air.

18

The best place for a polar bear to find its prey is at a hole in the ice, where the seals come up for air. The bear can tell by the smell whether a hole is in use. It stands perfectly still by the hole until a seal appears, and then knocks it out with a single blow of its paw. A polar bear can lift a 550-lb. (250-kg) seal out of the water with its jaws.

▼ The polar bear's food chain depends on a steady supply of the tiny swimming animals known as plankton.

POLAR BEAR FOOD CHAIN

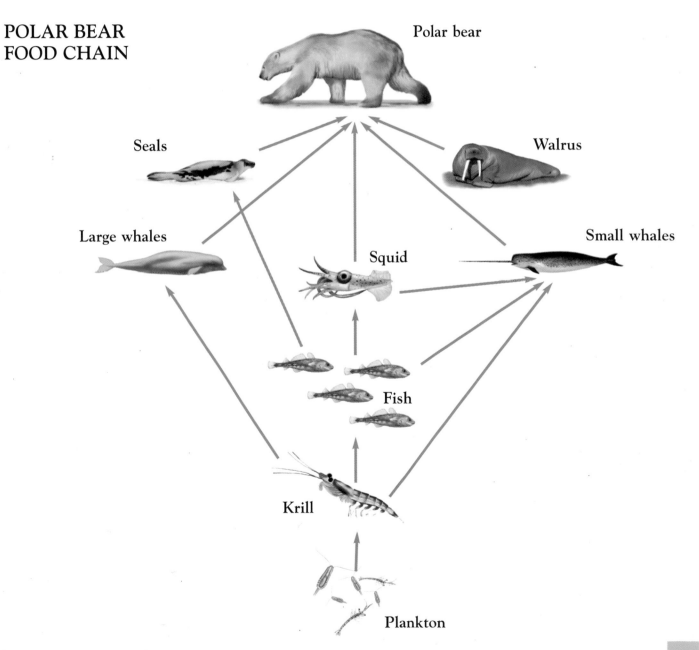

Polar bear

Seals

Walrus

Large whales

Squid

Small whales

Fish

Krill

Plankton

Stalking

Besides lying in wait, polar bears also stalk seals on the ice. They often catch hooded seals and harp seals as they bask on the ice. The bear creeps across the ice on its belly, using ridges and hills to hide behind until it is within about 65 ft. (20 m) —close enough to charge.

▼ Polar bears don't usually eat all that they kill. The leftovers are an important source of food for ivory gulls and Arctic foxes, which follow bears wherever they go. You can see a gull in this photo, waiting to have its share of the food.

EATING

Polar bears are very clean animals. After feeding on a kill, they wash themselves carefully in water or snow.

●

When a polar bear kills a seal, it eats only the intestines and the blubber under the skin.

► Once it has left its mother's lair, a young ringed seal has a better chance of escaping hungry polar bears.

In April and May, the bears hunt young ringed seals in their lairs under the snow. The mother seal digs the lair before her pup is born. The snow melts and refreezes around her, forming a hard crust of ice. When a polar bear sniffs out the lair, it jumps repeatedly on the ice with its front feet until the roof breaks. The seal pup has no chance of escape.

▲ Polar bears are excellent at swimming and diving. They can swim silently under-water, holding their breath, as they look for prey.

Other Foods

Polar bears eat other food besides seals. They kill small whales, such as narwhals and belugas, when they find them trapped in narrow leads in the ice. A group of bears in the Bering Sea once killed forty belugas and dragged them out onto the ice to eat.

Polar bears sometimes eat seaweed on the beach. At first, people thought it was because the bears were starving. But then they saw them diving to collect seaweed in the winter, when there was plenty of other food available. The seaweed contains vitamins that the bears may need to keep healthy.

In Canada's Hudson Bay, polar bears have been seen hunting ducks. They swim quietly underwater beneath a flock of ducks dabbling at the surface, and then bob up to grab them from below.

▼ These two polar bear cubs are digging out seaweed from under the snow.

Feeding in the Summer

In the summer, the ice melts and seals are harder to catch. Polar bears have to find other sources of food. They may patrol the beaches below seabird colonies, looking for fallen eggs and chicks. Sometimes they steal the eggs of eider ducks, which make their nests on the ground.

▼ Summer can be a hungry time for a polar bear. This bear is looking for food along the coast.

▲ An eider duck sits tight on her nest, relying on her camouflage to hide from polar bears and other predators.

Polar bears also hunt lemmings. They dig them out of their burrows or catch them on the surface. They also dig in the soil to find grass roots and plant tubers.

In a bad summer, a polar bear may have nothing to eat for weeks. Young cubs depend on their mother for milk all this time, but if she cannot find enough food, the whole family could die.

A mother polar bear suckles her cubs until they are at least twenty months old. In places where the climate is especially cold, she may look after them for another year.

When the cubs are weaned, the mother is ready to mate again and the cubs are driven away. They have to set out on their own and hunt for themselves. They will survive only if they have learned how to hunt well from their mother. Many cubs starve to death after leaving home.

▲ In driving snow, these two-year-old cubs need their mother if they are to survive.

▶ A mother bear waits for a seal to surface. She can smell its breath from the last time it surfaced.

Leaving Home

After leaving home, young bears spend most of their time on their own. They explore their new surroundings and learn to hunt. They do their best to avoid adult males, who would kill them. Only about four out of ten young bears survive their first winter. Most starve to death.

▲ Thin ice makes traveling difficult for a young bear alone in the frozen world.

▼ The size of a polar bear's range depends on how much food it contains. Where food is scarce, a single bear may roam more than 75,000 sq. mi. (195,000 sq. km).

Polar bears were once thought to wander the Arctic, traveling wherever they wanted. But scientists now think that each bear has its own home range. A young bear may travel more than 600 mi. (1,000 km) to set up a home range away from its mother. Home ranges often overlap, but they are usually so large that there is little chance of a young bear's meeting another of its kind.

Meeting and Greeting

When polar bears meet, it is usually at a large supply of food such as a dead whale. To avoid fights, they have a special way of greeting each other. The two bears circle each other, grunting quietly until they touch noses. They often begin sparring, to see which is the stronger. The weaker of the two soon realizes it would be dangerous to start a fight.

Although they are silent when they are alone, polar bears have a range of signals to tell others how they feel. They use a variety of grunts and growls, with angry hisses and threatening roars if they are injured.

▶ Young bears wrestle in play. At this age, they have nothing to fear from polar bear cubs of their own size.

▼ Two adult bears meet on the shore of Hudson Bay in Canada. After approaching each other cautiously, they touch noses in greeting.

30

Bears at the Dump

The most crowded population of polar bears in North America is around Hudson Bay, where between 100 and 150 cubs emerge from their dens each spring. When the sea-ice melts in the summer, they are joined by other bears until hundreds of them spread out across the landscape looking for food.

▼ Bear cubs forage in the town dump at Churchill, Manitoba, Canada. They are fearless and curious, but they may get sick from eating garbage.

POLAR BEARS AND PEOPLE

The tourist trade in Churchill, the "polar bear capital of world," brings in between two and three million dollars a year.

●

Polar bears can be playful as well as fierce. When one climbed aboard a Canadian Coast Guard vessel, the crew tried to drive it away with a powerful hose. But the bear enjoyed the shower, raising its front legs to let the water flow under its armpits.

▲ Inquisitive bears make great photo-opportunities for tourists.

Many bears gather to feed at the town dump in Churchill, Manitoba. Scavenging among the smouldering piles of garbage, the bears get scorched and filthy, so they are continually going to the sea to wash. Churchill is a favorite place to watch bears, because they are tame and easy to approach. The town has developed a thriving tourist industry based on the bears.

A Fully Grown Bear

Females usually have their first cubs when they are five or six years old. After that, they breed every three to four years until they are about twenty-one. Males are mature at three years, but few of them mate successfully until they are at least six.

◀ This adult bear stands almost 10 ft. (3 m).

ADULT POLAR BEARS

Male polar bears reach full size at eight to ten years old, and females at five or six. Both males and females can live to be about thirty years old.

A fully grown male measures 6 to 8 ft. (2–2.5 m) from nose to tail, and weighs 660 to 1,760 lbs. (300–800 kg). Adult females reach 6 to 6.5 ft. (1.8–2 m), and weigh 330 to 660 lbs. (150–300 kg).

▲ Longing to get back to its hunting grounds on the ice, a bear pants in the warm autumn sunshine.

Polar bears migrate with the seasons, always staying within reach of the edge of the ice. As the ice grows south in the winter, they move south. In the summer, when the ice melts again, the bears are forced north. Only pregnant females and their cubs live in dens throughout the winter. Other adults spend most of the winter roaming the ice.

Keeping Warm

Winter temperatures in the Arctic can be –58° F (–50° C) for days or weeks on end. Polar bears survive this bitter cold easily because their bodies are well insulated. Their thick coats trap warm air next to the skin, and under the skin is a layer of blubber that can be more than 4 in. (10 cm) thick.

In fiercely cold winds, a polar bear may dig a shelter in a snowbank. Then it curls up and waits for the wind to die down.

▲ A polar bear shelters from a storm in a hole it has dug in a bank of loose snow.

▼ Although this polar bear is running across the ice, polar bears rely on stealth, not speed, to catch their prey.

Polar bears lose very little body heat, even in the coldest weather. In fact, they are more likely to get too hot than too cold especially if they move too fast. This explains why polar bears usually walk quite slowly and rarely run very far.

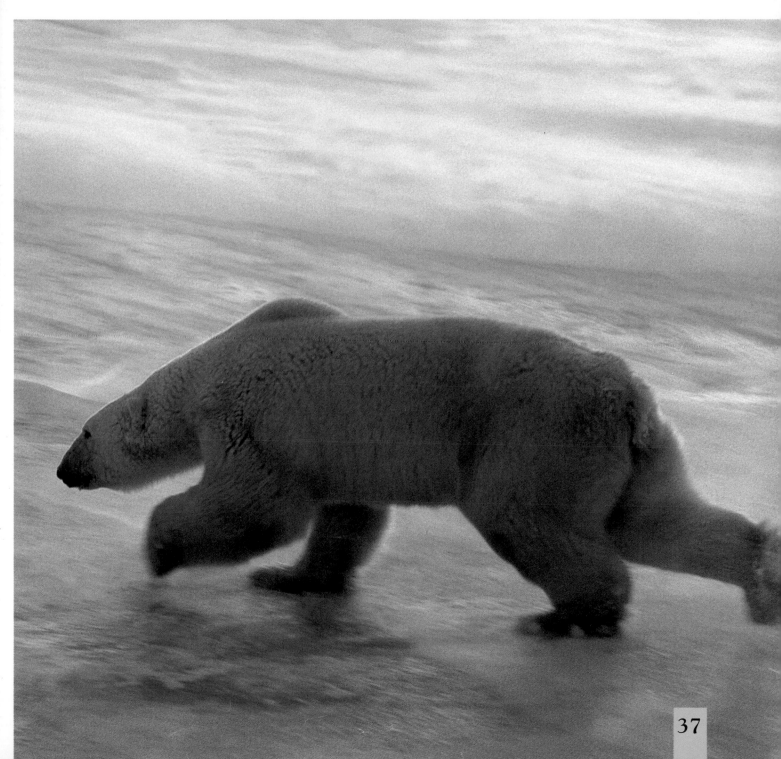

The Mating Season

Polar bears mate in late March to mid-May. Mature males can smell a female that is ready to mate from far away, and they will follow the scent until they find her. After mating, the male leaves.

If a male finds a female, he may kill her cubs, which will cause her to come into season so that he can mate with her.

During the mating season, rival males often challenge each other in disputes over females. Each fluffs out his coat to make himself look as big as possible. Males often swagger along, growling, to emphasize their size and weight. Polar bear researchers call this the "cowboy walk."

▶ With his coat fluffed out, a male bear performs the "cowboy walk" to scare off his rivals.

◀ The air is full of signals for a male polar bear, with his fine-tuned sense of smell.

Threats

An adult polar bear's only enemies are humans and, on rare occasions, other bears. The most serious threats caused by humans are the spread of oil and gas industries, pollution caused by toxic chemicals, and the effects of climate change. These all affect the polar bear's habitat.

▼ Offshore oil rigs can pollute the sea, threatening marine life not only in the Arctic but also throughout the world.

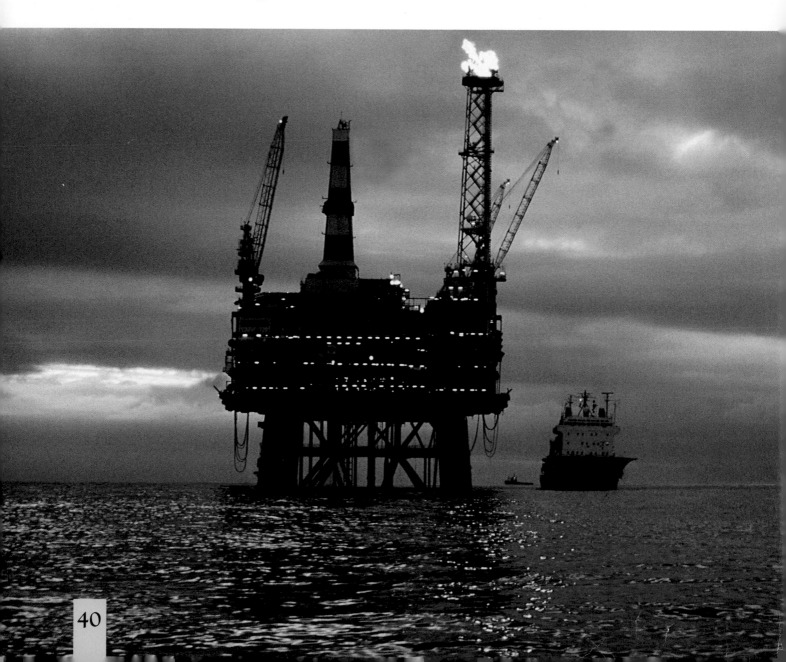

THREATS TO OTHER BEARS

Hunting, poaching, and habitat loss are the three main threats to other species of bears.

•

Bear hunting is allowed by some governments, to control the numbers in areas where there are too many bears.

•

Illegal poaching is done by hunters who sell body parts such as heads, furs, or paws for high prices.

•

Habitat loss happens as human populations grow and move into bear territories. The small bears that live in the tropics are threatened because the forests where they live are being cut down for lumber and to create new farmland.

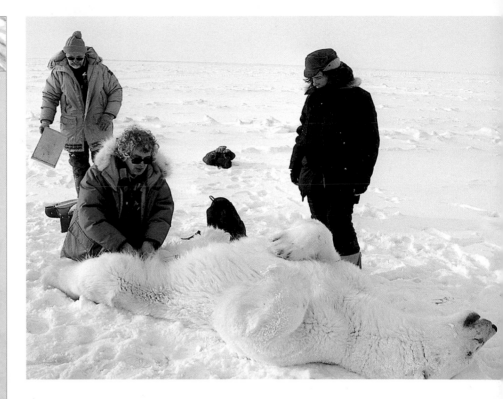

▲ Scientists take samples to check the level of pollution in a polar bear's blood. The bear has been put to sleep by a dart fired from a gun.

Drilling for oil and gas can cause pollution, which harms the bears and the creatures they hunt for food. Toxic chemicals are carried to the Arctic by the wind from industrial areas.

Because of global warming, some of the Arctic ice is melting and the bears have less space in which to live.

► This polar bear skin is being dried on a frame outside a house in northwestern Greenland.

◄ Native peoples are allowed to hunt polar bears for their own use. The Inuit around Thule in Greenland kill about 100 a year to make boots and pants for the winter.

Protecting Polar Bears

Inuit have hunted polar bears for thousands of years. Traditional hunting with spears did not harm the bear population as much as modern rifles do. Inuit are still allowed to kill some bears each year, mainly for their skins. A polar bear's skin is warm and waterproof—ideal for Arctic clothing.

Until the International Agreement on the Conservation of Polar Bears and their Habitat in 1973, hundreds of bears were killed each year by commercial hunters, who sold the skins. Hunting for sport or for money has now almost ceased. In the 1950s there were only about 5,000 polar bears. Today there are around 40,000, but it is difficult to count them accurately because they are so scattered.

On page 47 you will find a list of wildlife organizations helping to protect polar bears.

Polar Bear Life Cycle

1 Between one and four cubs (usually two) are born in their mother's den in December. She feeds them with milk. Their eyes open after thirty-three days.

2 In March, the cubs emerge from the den to follow their mother to the coast, where she hunts for seals.

3 The cubs lie quietly in the snow while their mother goes to find food for herself, to keep up her supply of milk.

4 The cubs spend their first winter with their mother. In their second year, they learn to hunt, though they are still being suckled by their mother.

 5 After leaving their mothers, polar bears spend most of their time on their own. When they meet others, they often play with each other.

 6 Females have their first cubs at five years old, but most males do not breed until they are six to eight. Both males and females can live to about thirty years old.

Glossary

Blubber A layer of fat under the skin.

Camouflage A way of avoiding notice by looking like the surroundings.

Carnivore A meat-eating animal.

Global warming The gradual warming of the earth's climate caused by pollution.

Hibernate To sleep through the winter.

Home range The area where an individual animal lives and hunts.

Ice floe A vast area of frozen sea.

Insulated Protected from the cold.

Inuit Native people of the Arctic regions of North America, Greenland, and Russia.

Krill Small, shrimplike creatures.

Lair A covered hole in the snow where a wild animal sleeps and gives birth.

Leads Spaces of clear water between ice floes.

Migrate To move from one place to another in search of food or warmer weather.

Plankton Microscopic plants and animals.

Prey An animal that is killed and eaten by another animal.

Scavenge To feed on dead animals, often those killed by another animal.

Sparring Fighting for practice or for fun.

Stalk To creep up on prey.

Suckle An animal suckles when it feeds on its mother's milk.

Toxic Poisonous.

Tuber The part of a plant stem that stores food underground. A potato is a tuber.

Tundra An open, treeless area in the Arctic.

Weaned Beginning to eat solid food rather than living on mother's milk.

Further Information

Organizations to Contact

Center for Environmental Education
1725 DeSales Street NW
Suite 500
Washington, DC 20036

Friends of the Earth (U.S.A.)
218 D Street SE
Washington, DC 20003

Greenpeace U.S.A.
1436 U Street NW
Washington, DC 20009

Nature Conservancy
1815 N. Lynn Street
Arlington, VA 22209

World Wildlife Fund
1250 24th Street NW
Washington, DC 20037

Web Sites

The Bear Den
www.nature-net.com/bears/
polar.html
This site has information and pictures of polar
bears, and links to sites about other bears.

Polar Bears Alive
www.polarbearsalive.org/
Facts, news and pictures. This site is run by a non-
profit organization dedicated to preserving the
Arctic environment.

Books to Read

Brown, Gary. *The Great Bear Almanac*. New York:
Lyons & Burford, 1993.

Herrero, Steven. *Bear Attacks: Their Causes and
Avoidance*. New York: Nick Lyons Books, 1985.

Lynch, Wayne. *Bears*. Vancouver: Douglas &
McIntyre, 1993.

Penny, Malcolm. *The Polar Seas* (Seas and Oceans).
Austin, TX: Raintree Steck-Vaughn, 1997.

Pollack, Steve. *Atlas of Endangered Animals*. New
York: Facts on File, 1993.

Stirling, Ian, ed. *Bears: Majestic Creatures of the
Wild*. New York: Rodale Press, 1993.

Taylor, Barbara. *Arctic and Antarctic*. New York:
Knopf Books for Young Readers, 1995.

Index

All the numbers in **bold** refer to photographs or illustrations.

Arctic foxes 20

birth 10, 44
black bears 7
blubber 5, 20, 36, 46
brown (grizzly) bears **7**

camouflage 4, **25**, 46
coat and fur 4, 5, 36

dens 8, **9**, 10, 11, 13, 35, 44
ducks 23, 24, **25**

ears and hearing 5, 11
eyes 5, 44

feet and claws 5
fighting 16, 30
food and feeding 4, 11, 14, 15, 17, **18**, **19**, **20**, 22, **23**, **24**, 25, **29**, 30, 32, 33, 44

growling 30, 38

home ranges 29, 46
hunting 16, **18**, 19, 25, 26, **27**, 28, 43, 44, 45, 46

Inuit **42**, 43, **43**, 46

jaws 19

lemmings 25

mating 34, 38
milk **11**, 14, 25, 44

playing **12**, 13, 32, 45
pregnancy 8, 35

resting **13**, **15**, **17**, **35**

seabirds 24
seals 18, 19, 20, **21**, 22, 24, 44, 46
sense of smell 5, **17**, 19, **27**, 30, 38
skin 5, **43**
sparring 30, 31, 46
spectacled bears 7
stomachs 4
suckling **11**, 26, 45, 46
swimming 6, **22**, 23

tourists 32, **33**

walruses 18, 19
warmth (how bears keep warm) 4, 5, 11, 36, 37
whales 5, 18, 19, 22, 30, 46